21 Thoughts

Melissa Koenig

21 Thoughts © 2022 Melissa Koenig

All rights reserved.

No part of this publication may be reproduced, stored in a retrieval system, or transmitted, in any form or by any means, electronic, mechanical, photocopying, recording or otherwise, without the prior written permission of the presenters.

Melissa Koenig asserts the moral right to be identified as author of this work.

Presentation by *BookLeaf Publishing*

Web: www.bookleafpub.com

E-mail: info@bookleafpub.com

ISBN: 9789357618410

First edition 2022

For my number one fan, my Mumma!

You have been there since day one and are proud of anything I do. You have kept many scraps of paper I have written on, and all those moments of writing have led to this book. Thank you for your unwavering support. x

ACKNOWLEDGEMENT

Thank you to my partner Jason, the only person who knew I was taking on this project. I am without many words for what it means to me to have your support. Allowing me space to be my own, weird self and never questioning why or how I do anything. Even if you don't understand something I do, you never judge me, which allows me to live in happiness. The best place to be and I get to share it with you. x

PREFACE

By no means would I call myself a writer, let alone a poet. However I have 'written' so must be a writer. I have 'poeted' so I am a poet. I made that up, and that has been the fun of writing these poems. Making them up. Not giving myself any rules to abide by just free writing and editing…a little.

The challenge given was to write 21 poems in just 21 days and that is not much time! With real life thrown in between, the poems were never going to be refined, but the rawness and lack of time to reconsider the thoughts was a draw card. I dared myself to take a chance and give purpose to the words that swirl in my head, usually meaninglessly. So here they are, published. I have published a book...just had to put that in writing as the thought of it is surreal.

Yellow

In a world left dark
A legacy is sought
In yellow

Scraps of memories
Torn from consciousness
Sewn into a tribute

To envelope in warmth
And create light
In spite of the dark

Pillow

Her scent
My pillow
Transcends her presence

Drenched in heat
With an uncontrolled grin
Memories play like a movie preview

A feature film never produced
A script I play over in my head

T-shirt

His scent
His T-shirt
Transcends his presence

Drenched in warmth
With an uncontrolled smirk
Memories play like a movie preview

A feature film never produced
A script I play over in my head

The Truth

To lie
Or to lie
Next to him
In sin

The truth
Not hidden
Blazed
On my skin

Vintage

She wears vintage
One of a kind

She feels vintage
Marked with time

She is vintage
Better with age

Gorgeous

Damn, he has no idea

The crease in his cheek
as he naturally smiles

The curls in his hair
as they naturally fall

The lines on his torso
as he naturally stands

The curve of his butt
as he naturally lays

Good morning gorgeous

Hot Car

Pull up to my driveway
Beep the horn
Throw open your door
I'm good to go

Pull away
Rubber peeling
Big grin and
a little giggle

I don't care
where we go
Just that I'm with you

Reckless freedom
This moment
the road...

...and you

All You

Time is
all I give you

I chose
you to give it to

Far from forever

Filling a moment
or a whole Friday night

Filling a desire
or a new interest

Filling a curiosity
or a shared want

But never filling
the space of forever

Rose Tinted Glasses

If you could
see what I see
Wear the lenses
like I do

You'd see the
beauty in the world
And you would
smile too

Sneans

A sight you
can't unsee

A sneaker
and a jean

Laced up
New Balance sneaks

or maybe a pair
of coloured Asics

Takes a certain
type of man

To rock the look
like he can

Island Paradise

My happy place
One like no other

A tattoo on my heart
The pilgrimage calls

Two wheels rolling
And the island is home

93

Marc
etched on my skin

Marc
imprinted in history

Marc
engraved on the MotoGP world

Marc
stamped as a legend

Sometimes

I still think you're here
sometimes
Like I could call
and you would answer
Drive my car
to your house
And you'd roll out
a cigarette, a smile, a high five

I still see you here
sometimes
Like you're standing
right in front of me
I wait for you to
help me
And you show me signs
a fortune, a bird, a breeze

I still hear you here
sometimes
Like in moments I know
you'd have something to say
Driving in my car
on a highway
And your voice plays
a remark, a quote, a song

Daddy-O

I feel you in my heart
I hear you in my head
Gone from this painful world
But so far from dead

Felicity

For all the wonder in the world
the beauty that I see
Nothing is more beautiful
than you are to me

Waves

Staring at my toes
like I've never seen them before
Waiting for the moment
water bubbling over

Tension drops from my body
falling through the sand
Salty breeze whipping my hair
undoing all worry held within

Each step closer to release
the chill stabs
I dip my head back
surrendering to the sea

Blaze

A cherry pop eye
her cuteness prevails
Blazy-Blaze cutie pie

Dancing

Like food
it fuels me

Best served hot
simmering on the plate

Too hot to touch
but tasty enough to watch

Hair

Single strands dropped

A piece of me

Breadcrumbs trailing
swept up in the breeze
or into a corner

Carried through time
travelling beyond
but once part of me

Books

We shared more than a sentence
but perhaps
only merely a page
printed in history

As you write your
next chapter
I will no longer be there
to spark your story

In chapters
I can't bear to read
and couldn't borrow
from a library if I wanted

Your life goes on
without your heroine
and maybe I'll be there
for a flashback of better days

I can only hope
my hero is yet to be found
but for you without me
your story is a plot without intrigue

Printed in the USA
CPSIA information can be obtained
at www.ICGtesting.com
LVHW011540050124
767941LV00091B/5154